The Bloomsberries
and Other Curiosities

The Bloomsberries
and Other Curiosities

Poems by

Laurie Byro

Kelsay Books

Cover art:
Painting by Michael Byro "Virginia Woolf in Pointillism"

ISBN: 13-978-1-945752-66-7

Kelsay Books
Aldrich Press
www.kelsaybooks.com

In memory of my father, Paul Dwight Lampe,
nature's aristocrat.

Acknowledgments

The author would like to thank the judges and editors of venues where the following poems first appeared, some in earlier forms:

Autumn Sky Poetry Daily: "Comrade"
Chronogram: "After My Grandmother's Love Letters,"
    "The Snow Angel"
The Galway Review: "A Tale of Canterbury," "Conquest,"
    "Lady Macbeth's Ambitions," "The Gamekeeper's Forest,"
    "The Red King," "The White Queen"
Hobo Camp Review: "Woodcock"
Illya's Honey: "Sunflowers"
Interboard Poetry Community, reprinted in *Luna* (Aldrich Press,
2015)*:* "Virginia Sings Back to the Stones in her Pockets"
Loch Raven Review: "Madame Cezanne With Unbound Hair
    (1869)"
New Jersey Journal of Poets: "Lazarus Receives a Visit From His
    Sister Mary," "Shipwrecked in a Reel of Stars," "Stones for the
    Apostles." Honorable Mention: NJ Poet's Prize
Pirene's Fountain: "Oracle," "Silk Routes"
Right Hand Pointing, reprinted at *Verse Virtual:* "Candle Lion"
*South Florida Poetry Journal (*with Audio*):* Part 3 of The Goose
    Girl, "The Rival"
Synchronized Chaos: "April in Moscow," "Virginia's
    Constellations"
THAT Literary Review: "Snow in Wind," "Incubus"
The Legendary, Down and Dirty Word: "Conquest"
Verse Virtual: "The Green Woman," "The Peacock"
Wonder: "The Dream Fox"
Worm 38: "Vineyard Nature"

Contents

Some people go to priests; others to poetry;
I to my friends.
                    —Virginia Woolf

PART I: The Bloomsberries

I impose nothing, I propose nothing, I expose.
—Lytton Strachey

*The Bloomsbury Group lived in squares,
painted in circles, and loved in triangles.*
—Dorothy Parker

Virginia's Constellations

Whatever actually happened at Yang-ping's house
during that winter, there were seasons before and after

in which nothing happened. Rowboats skiffled along
rain-washed river bottoms, rocky but not impassable.

There wasn't always a drunken moon or salty stars
in a black bowl of sky. A heron followed the boat

seeking clues about the lady in the wide-brimmed hat,
a blue ribbon trailing the wind like its mate's feathers.

The tail of Scorpio slashed the wild sky. The woman
blinded by icy stars, could have been mistaken for a wizened

"Chinaman," thousands of years old. The silent river spilled
no secrets about temptation or regret. The woman who navigated

these waters held a compass that could turn her boat around,
change to any direction. She planted her long legs solidly

on its wooden floor, a book open and faced down
beside her written by a man who'd traveled similar waters.

Many winters before, too many to record in a hand-painted chart,
Li Po paddled a river, his oars dripping stars.

Stones for the Apostles

Against you I will fling myself, unvanquished and unyielding,
O Death.

—Virginia Woolf

There were stones for skimming, they parted the watery sheets
of her suicide like the palms of God, she had rehearsed them

for years, practicing their music. She summoned them like tongues
of the apostles as they announced her arrival. Like God, she had

chosen a Jew; she didn't believe in him exactly. Stones beckoned
her through these gates of the sacred Jews. She employed them

like soldiers, heavy and round, beautiful as spring potatoes,
she'd divide them into each pocket, there were always plenty

to share. This river kneaded them like bread, she would leave
a trail. As she sank down deeper into the brackish waters of her

imagination, *down down*, touching bottom at last, she planted them
like a nest of eggs. They were gorgeous, a man's hidden body,

this terror of the unknown, only took her under for moments,
this cool lover's embrace, she had anticipated this end

her entire life. She is a vessel emptying herself of words,
the burden of her skin, the first awkward sentence, a last vowel

escaping her mouth churning to the surface of the River Ouse.
How beautiful she shudders. *My soul now this river, free at last.*

Virginia Sings Back to the Stones in Her Pockets

I must get the details right. How stones warbled
to her from the garden for a fortnight or so. Troublesome,
intrusive, they trilled while she weeded anemones. Beneath
the ease of roots and thrust of new growth, they ingratiated

themselves to her prodding callused fingers. They knew
her sister was the lucky one, the one who skimmed flat-brimmed
lake stones with the children. This one lay on the couch
with her eyelids peeled back, mushroom capped stones rattling

in the crèche of her eye sockets. Stones were faithful as vowels;
they didn't let her down. Night after night, her husband begged
her to push them back into the gully of silence. Last night,
she overturned another patch of fertile earth, brushing

off the smooth and round. She pictures the summer table noisy
with anemones and her sister's brood. She is washed out, a little
brown thrush. "Drab hen, frump" her sister will urge her to over-
come the day's exacting brushes. I must get the colors right,

melt down her charms to the bare-bone mauves and ochre.
The stones will do their job shortly. Aggressive reds need to be
given back to the soil—to the bridegroom river. We must empty
out all the flecked mica chips from her pockets, the cloth's blood
stained lullabies, the stones' last sweet songs.

Leonard Woolf's Heaven

One must be crucified on one's private cross.
—Leonard Woolf

Even my lifetime hand tremor, marked me somehow chosen
to fulfill an understudy's role in their petty dramas.

I was always essential to them, though not as driven by a spark
of divine fire by those wise virgins. Someone told me once

I looked like an old Testament prophet, so I picked Elijah,
not bad for an atheist. For me heaven was an unruly Ceylon

jungle, that messy bride's bed. Like my love for Virginia,
the jungle surged forward and blotted the walls of their huts.

It made our lives less important for the whole. My love-breath
was hot and heavy, an animal thrashing through shrubs and bushes,

trees. The disorder of the jungle was like madness, thorns
and creepers suffocating rice-fields and healthy soil. If it had not

been for love, we would have hardly mattered. If it had not been
for me, she would have sacrificed herself sooner than she did.

Heaven for Lytton

If this is dying, then I don't think much of it.
—Lytton Strachey

Naturally, I am not surprised to find Victoria and Albert among my
fellow travelers and he, finally out in the open, no longer faithful

to her. Well, I suspect in this realm we are no longer devoted to
anything, quite? All these dead soldiers, if I objected then, I

certainly object now, what a waste of breath. To dedicate oneself to
a capitalist war, simply to preserve an empire is madness. Here,

most are Conchies, and as this is heaven after all, most of the men,
like me have beards, gloriously tinted all shades. I spend my days in

contemplation of their sultry beauty. We look like decadent French
poets; I am free to wander, at least until Carrington comes. I have

given up writing for a time, and bask in their heady cinnamon
skin, obliged to all the delights that my fine life has afforded.

Heaven for John Maynard Keynes

Nothing mattered except states of mind, chiefly our own. The
clocks cannot be set back.

—Keynes

After living a life of $Y = C + 1$, saving for the future, spending
and investing, blissfully eating, drinking, and other pursuits

of revelry, I can tell you that for me heaven existed under my feet
as well over my head, and it's not much different here as the life

I lived, fully and completely before. Here's a fact you'll snigger
at because it is so obvious, but it is a point I need make now.

The pursuit of money for its own sake is a pathological condition—
the proper aim of work is to provide leisure. That is what it's about,

that is the goal and end, the future and the present, and it shouldn't
take a wise man, an economist or a fool to reiterate this.

And since you'll ask, my wife with her foxy lips, did indeed sit
in the refrigerator (naturally with the doors open, sensible girl)

completely nude and make no mistake, fully and entirely with
my encouragement. What a treat to find her thus, in that damnable

Washington heat, the only way to cool down, a practical,
economical thing to do: a taste of real heaven before the final call.

Afterwards for Clive Bell

Art and Religion are, then, two roads by which men escape
from circumstance to ecstasy.

—Clive Bell

Studying at Cambridge, I smuggled a reproduction Degas
along with my hunting horn and twelve-bore cartridges
in my luggage. Now, I am suffering for the part my family

played in it. All the abused miners, all the wild animals shot
to give us a status worth having, a bride worth sharing. A lion
skin, or tiger skin, and some imitation paintings, are they

the symbols of a life? On the Savannah, a bleeding queen will seek
a strong male, will shun the frail or weak. Yes, I have had
sunny days in tall grass, but nothing prepared me for losing

Vanessa, the single most failure of my life. Had I to do it over,
I would have surely changed. All that time I never appreciated
the real for the faux until it was too late and we were gone.

What Duncan Grant Thought

Shall I part my hair behind? Do I dare to eat a peach?
I shall wear white flannel trousers, and walk upon the beach.
                                                    —T.S. Eliot

No matter what they say about me, the Duke of Devonshire, once
called me "impishly benign" and so I've tried to live thus,
the elephant's way: huge in all things, my appetites never ending,

nor the loves of my life. I wasn't convinced I should father a child,
Vanessa ever an earth-mother, talked me into it. A messy business,
I shall die not knowing if that were a mistake, but rather than create

havoc, I created a child. Oh, my personality may have outshone
my paintings, I hope not. Lytton would say I was Puck in our merry
band of buggers, Vanessa, The Fairy Queen. But this I believe as I

once wrote from a Bazaar at Smyrna "the camels, the cries,
the colors, the mysteries." That note from Turkey could have been
a postcard summing up my life. I would have traveled forever

with that chap. We passed through strange and shaggy interludes,
then he breathed no more. Lytton never lived to hear the Beatles.
I did, and I was in many ways all four of them, fascinated with

friends and interests. I lived my life without a moral philosophy,
as such, studied GE Moore's principles. I was never a drunk man
examining thistle. As a result, I accepted people as they were, not

desiring anything from them, other than acceptance. For forty years,
I lived happily with our benign Goddess Vanessa, my truest friend,
who encouraged me to be the only thing I could be, that is myself.

Heaven for Desmond MacCarthy

It's no secret I was the favorite of the "Bloomsberries" as Mollie
called us, a Cambridge Apostle who taught them well.
Of anyone, it seemed, I was destined for success. I made it

my business to show, by example, that earning a life was indeed
more important than earning a living. When I began coming to
the Friday club, I felt the Miss Stephens were looking like slaves.

Equality is a dangerous thing, the power lies in resistance.
Money, too, is fraught with disappointment, lucky I had little,
except what I needed: an easy chair, a fine fire, reams of paper

just waiting for me to transform them, coy virgins, blank
unadorned pages into a novel: a perfect petulant paradise.
Often, I was told I would be the next Henry James.

I was simply waiting, for "the Title" of my beloved to appear.
I had charmed and domesticated English language.
I had put my British maiden on a leash. Heaven for me, would be

to wake up, astonished, with a perfectly bound (and gagged)
volume of perfect prose, a Midsummer's Friday-night dream.
Naturally, with Duncan casting spells as Puck did, an angelic

chorus consisting of the Stephens, dear Mollie and poor Dora,
singing tra la la, la la. If only we could win this plot
against the giant. And me, merrily recording it all, warmed by

those dove's wings as they encouraged me, not
as a journalist, but as an important man of letters, someone
to pay attention to: the father of them all.

What Morgan Thought

Death destroys a man: the idea of Death saves him.
—EM Forster

The first time I heard a man sing was attending
a Red Cross soldier in Egypt. I lost my virginity to him.

Later, he died. They all go into silence, yet we cannot
help assigning them a tune. *Sing, sing, my dear hearts,*

come stomp on the porch, awaken me with song.
After I lost R, I became obsessed with le petit mort.

I had stopped thinking of the dead evenly. It began
with a hum, and then became a crescendo.

I heard it tiptoe down the badge of a cop about to fall.
I heard the whistle of a bullet, at first irritating

but then an invitation, a summons. I hear it now,
the click, click of teeth and tongue, the waiting more

unbearable than the music, a hurdy-gurdy lion's roar.
The crackle of heat rising off a dry sand road, off

the dung of a camel, glorious crackle, another angel
about to fall. The moan and gasp as trees rub

their fronds, to quote my friend Tom "I have heard
the mermaids singing, each to each.

I do not think they will sing to me." Most of whom
I have known leave no sound behind. I cannot evoke them

though I would like to. Yes, I would hope I have
the guts to betray my country but not my friend.

I shall face these charges, and more. My tenet is this:
only connect, connect only. Lonely? Connect.

A Casket for Roger Fry

Art is significant deformity.
                    —Roger Fry.

I will not forget her hands
when she traced her love-words onto my shoulders,
So suitably now my life is over,
That I am quietly hers.

When she traced her love-words onto my shoulders
I saw an honest man pass before my eyes.
My life is over, that I am quietly hers.
I tried to tell her there and then.

My kingdom, all my paintings for this touch.
So suitably now my life is over.
I tried to tell her there and then
I will not forget her hands.

She brought me garlands, rain and snowy kisses
and painted sunny days that we had seen.
I filled the night with us and all our wishes.
The days and nights dissolved upon our tongue.

She painted sunny days that we had seen.
A kind of daring, a perpetual daydream.
The days and nights dissolved upon our tongue.
Her brush was her magic, she painted me holy.

A kind of daring, a perpetual daydream.
I filled the night with us and all our wishes.
Her brush was her magic, she painted me wholy.
She brought me garlands, rain and snowy kisses.

Madame Cézanne with Unbound Hair (1869)

You parted the cool braid
of my hair, it snaked like rain along your shoulder.
Early autumn: yellow leaves laid
a pattern of eyes at our window. Colder
weather would cower them into cones
and we would sit crossed-legged on the bed
each uncurling the other like a fortune teller's hand. Poems
didn't hold us as much as time passing. We read
to one another. You told me my hair
was a fragile ladder, we needed to escape
the turbulent green rivers that dared
to take us under. You kissed the nape
of my neck and spun out the coils of golden brown.
We practiced an ancient tapestry, the art form we found.

Still Life with Self-Portrait (1918)

By my ambitions, I am cut off from my family and class . . .
So I am an outcast.

—Mark Gertler

Always on the wedding canvas,
a portrait of taupe and grey:
my eyes focus on those things
you cannot see. From the lonely place
hacked between our mother's thighs
I was the last to fall,
a glistening gold coin.

I surround myself, a mirror of rage
and lift myself out of this room
and into sleepy trees.
A discontented owl, mouse entrails
smolder inside my veins,
as I walk I carve birch messages to her.

A Japanese stranger looms grim,
a creature alien as breath;
she is a distant rumble of train,
a far-off hymn. I lie in a mossy bed
with the tangled ribbons of my magic.

But like a polished stone, I slip
through the torn cloth of her pocket,
through her clumsy fist, and skitter
over, under and away,

Mountain Church Larrau

I cried to think of a savage cynical fate which had made it
impossible for my love ever to be used by you.
                                        —Dora Carrington

You wanted me to make it come out differently.
The chambers of a nautilus shell with its shady pink
spirals was as close I could get to painting light

as it came through the bleak church windows.
You told me my perspective was flawed. My strokes
were a dull parade of color but somehow I'd lost

the skill. I couldn't capture September yellow.
I couldn't be compared to the madman of Arles. The artist
lived inside sunflowers and could carve chasms into paint.

Watcher-crows bored holes into his heart. His brother's
letters whispered *not good enough,* the way you do with me.
As consolation I deny myself memory. Soon you'll forget

the boy with the purple birthmark, the leaf that spreads
across his face like the slap of a hand. I ask you
to explain the bitterness you say I cannot understand.

The painter waits on a stone step in a tattered white shirt.
The yellow dust of his house circles his throat
like a gold chain. Birds litter the stubble in their black mourning

coats. I think he wanted to stir himself into something else,
the purest blend of pigment. I want my scars to fall like seeds
into a field, to grow into sunflowers, to make you, Crow, healed.

The Dream Fox

The Bloomsburys are little swarming selves, I imagine crushing them.

—D.H. Lawrence

In the year 1918, there was not much food to buy.
The youth stole the dark eyes of the fox. The youth
had fallen from the dark eyes of the fox. When

he lifted his clouded blue-eyes, she remembered
the rabbit and wild duck flying high towards the wood,
that he had shot. Again, there was silence.

A cunning little flame came across the youth's face.
A gleam of red fed the fine hairs on his cheeks.
She put away the thought of him. He walked

towards the wood's edge with his gun. The youth
had stolen the dark eyes of the fox. He was
the Master of the girl. He would catch her as you catch

a deer or wood cock when you go out to shoot.
It became like a fate. The girl had fallen from
the dark eyes of the deer.

Daunsinge

after T.S. Eliot

Only those who will risk going too far
can possibly find out how far one can go.
—T.S. Eliot

In that open field of weak pipe and summer drum.
You can hear them dancing, nourishing the corn.
The time of harvest, earth feet, loam feet, moss
and mayhem: wait and summon the early owl.

In daunsinge, signifying matrimony, coupling
of woman and man, man and man rustically solemn
or in rustic laughter. Mirth of those that entered
the ground before. Milking the constellations,

dancing the living seasons, arms rising and falling,
leaping through the bonfire, fetish animals snarl
and nip, keep rhyme to their daunsinge. Do not
come close, do not stir this freeing fire.

Leaving Monk's House

The girls will have the table set
on its splintered French farm wood,

each sparrow weaves its ribbony nest
with the scraps from the table. Leave me,
in peace, Apostles, I shall say as I scrape

my boots free of silt and leave them outside
the door. The dented leather barks its own

tale. Tonight, we'll redeem ourselves
with a stingy, goodnight kiss. The flowers
are hushed, then silenced in their sticky blue-

moon purpose. We are petals curled; reflections,
lies, crushed in our fists. Inside a cavern

of glass, roots drag me down with their soft mitts
of clay. Guilty, you are all left clinging
to my toes. How many mouths will open

and close in wonder like the fish I've seen,
after I tell you just where I've been.

Note:
On March 28, 1941, Virginia Woolf loaded her pockets
with stones and drowned herself in the River Ouse.

Charleston Farmhouse

after Milosz

The fields were covered in star-frost as we returned
at day-break. Red wings with their crimson feathers

parted the dark. Suddenly a pair of foxes startled
the horses. One of our group alerted the others by

waving his hand. Forever, a long time ago, I remember.
Now none of them are alive, not the foxes,

nor the man who hushed the crunch of star-frost, nor
his horse. Loves, what has become of them?

The ribbons of light and fur, the rustle of cold
morning air, the mist off the horse's sleek heads.

I ask not in sorrow, yesterday is yesterday still.
I ask not in sorrow, but in inexplicable awe.

PART II: Other Curiosities

Curiouser and curiouser! Cried Alice (she was so much surprised, that for the moment she quite forgot how to speak good English).

—Lewis Carroll

Vineyard Nature

From the porch, Nathaniel watches
a woman by a window through thick
and wavy glass. She picks bits of thread
through a cloth with her sturdy needle.
She nips a strand with her teeth.
The crisscross of the curve of letter
unravels, cardinal reds, scarlet purple.

He writes her strong and straight
like the oak outside his door. No bend
to her, she will bow, she will not break.
A foghorn interrupts his pen. He loves her
black-eyed warble, the spidery line
that resolves her mouth as he passes her
on the street. She is round as an oyster,

her baby will be a pearl. The seed
she carries will be a speck of sand
in the fathers' eyes. A gull shrieks and chases
her worn gray skirts. He places a period
at the end of a long sentence.

While on a winter walk, Nathaniel discovers
a white-bleached skeleton of a baby cormorant.
He notes the bones that make up its wings,
the resiliency of pursuit and flight.

Eliza won't marry him, but he doesn't know
that yet. He'll only make love to her
on crisp sheets of white paper.

Incubus

To try and knit the bones of a child,
I leave sugar cubes on our windowsill.

Robins peck them to dust, peck the blue
right out of your eyes. I steal the eggs

of jays. I sip delicate shells clean
through the membrane, yellow with suns.

I weave feathers into my hair.
I clip it down to the scalp, invite

all predators to rob each shank, to spin
a nest with my leavings. Now, when

I carry groceries up to the door, I tear
the bags into ribbons to tie in my thrush

brown hair. I am no longer sure that
an egg with blood in it needs to be curdled

into paint when I smear each breast
with an orchid, with a sunrise. I swill

shadows and rain down my parched throat,
flood my mouth with a curse. I leave worms

thick with blood back on my windowsill
to be borrowed, to be used up.

Mother of Pearl

I was her secret like the scarlet thread,
I was her shame and her joy. I was the plastic purse

she held against her chest. She filled me with herself,
ravished me with her moon-changes. The fangs

and hooves scared me when I fell asleep. She transformed
me into a witch bottle from all her disappointments. She

poured me into a broken vase, filled it with orchid bulbs
and still it grew nothing. Later she cracked us open, sloughed

us into rust. Around us grew glistening shell, we
luminesced and acquiesced, but never were enough.

I have sealed my own and dragged my mermaid
rags up to her frothy night dress, her lengthy gasp.

She has been gone these ten years,
but never wholly in our grasp.

Sunflowers

for Aunt "Toots"

Other than watching sunflowers grow tall and bend
low, old peasants working the soil, I can't tell you how
I spent the summer. Every line I wrote, I crossed over,

all my mistakes erupted into bare spots on each
gold-fringed face. Bees flocked to my tow-haired children
making me believe there was never any deprivation.

Labor Day chrysanthemums split open a black kettle of sky.
Weary crone heads could be cut off and dried. I bundled
sunflowers and hung them upside down from the porch ceiling.

At night they sighed from their nooses. My father, alone
for the first time, slept in our spare bedroom. I cut each down
one at a time to give him pillow after pillow of sunflower.

By morning clutching coffee sweet and light in clay, he said
that the night before he had dreamt of his own true love.
Never once did I want to know her name.

The Snow Angel

My father, who dies on the longest night of the year, returns
a month later, somehow fifty three years old, a wild-eyed charmer,
to tell me that the dead aren't worrying about the living, that

each snowflake falling is a wish spoken before it hits the earth.
I am half awake, I rub my eyes. He stamps the porch, begging for
a decent cup of coffee, saying he has no rest for all those wishes,

no sleep for all those mad-rushes to pull us safely
to the curb. I am skeptical. I hand him his coffee: milk, no sugar.
He has that sheepish grin, that wolf-sure twinkle. *"Tell me*

you aren't disappointed dad, show me how you know
it's all ok." He guffaws his coffee. *"I would sleep like the dead.*
Instead, I have dervish-toddlers, toothless men. Mostly I have you.

Lighten up, they say, winter's my busy season." I blink, his cup
is empty, I was about to make us tea. His shoes wait by his empty
bed, Goodwill is coming next month. Each day I walk through

a forest with somebody's name carved on a tree. All winter, during
long feathery nights, wishes swirl round the house, falling
on the neighborhood, on the chimneys while we sleep.

Candle Lion

after Richard Brautigan

My porch in candles hosts all the lions who growl
from the other side. My father shoos raccoons

off the stairs. Last summer, he tossed a shovel
of gravel at a hungry bear. He could scare shadow-mice,

make darkness shiver. He pounces through
the candle's fire as it licks the waxy stars that fall.

We are white light, candle lions who belong
to the same pride. The heat of his breath sears

though he is no longer alive. I have nothing to fear from this
or that side. These candles have ancient amber eyes.

Snow in Wind

Years ago, the sculptor finished
with her. When he lit winter candles,

adorned her with ice he became an Eskimo,
chanting all the words for snow.

Snow fell while he explained this,
making me glisten, making me dissolve

 like a snowflake on his tongue.
Wind howled and wrapped itself around

our cabin in shrouds of fresh ice.
Inside, the sculptor carved moonlight.

His hands formed new bones for me.

A Tale of Canterbury

In Canterbury, my bicycle tires are scuffed
from cobblestones that in turn break apart moss
that grows in between. Each morning, I peddle
past a woman who tries to dissolve me like salt
into her husband's soup. He gathers
utensils: knives and stirrers to go off to work.

He pinches the air as he passes, blows a kiss
through the mist off sun-drying earth as it rises.
They grow peppery beans that she snaps and tears
then mixes into their evening broth. I sit at a table
outside his café day after day. I notice he has an extra
finger on each hand. After a week of lunches,

I have gathered enough familiarity to ask.
I read his palms as an excuse to examine
his oddness. I sniff each Mount of Venus—
he has water hands, his lines are a little naïve.
One day I ask for a knife and hack off one before
he can protest to plant as a souvenir in my garden.

He screams louder than the whistle on my homebound
train. Alone at night, I beg St. Augustine if this man's
will is free, or I freed it with my knife. The last time
I see him, he removes his ring and threads it through
the chain that hangs round my neck. It brushes
the pulse on my throat like a fingernail. Then,

something deep and guilty rises through me. I watch
his cool grey eyes fill like a cloud. Before I go back
to my room to pack I plant a row of sunflowers in their
yard under the black beads of a crow. She watches
me through the window, moves the curtains
with claws that no longer grow.

The Gamekeeper's Forest

after D.H. Lawrence

Old friends, Mellors loved the forest when
you were young. The grey eyes of the forest shut
its lids, remembering. This time of year, frost lay

mossy and blue in the cracks, mice hid
in the crevices of stone walls. Rheumy eyes

blur the edges loose. We are no longer held captive
to the boundaries of skin. Tight patches
of blackness hover where greenman fires

were lit. I summon trees to recall floaters and moats
as forest dust stirs and settles. Through the bracken

and oaks, the heart of England rests. Dense and bony
branches fill a cemetery of trees. There is no one alive
who remembers the deer and archers, the monks padding

along on asses. Trees in their hooded robes guard birds
who safely flit among them. This forest remembers,

still it remembers. Brushwood soot clings
to the brown hems of trees. A parade of trees,
like ghostly monks, honor their vow of silence.

Woodcock

Maybe it rained all night. In the morning,
the sea, brackish and choppy, fences your ride.
Words whistle in your ears, twenty-five miles
from home. You come across a woodcock,
dead, dropped from an envious ocean wind.
You spread its wing in the holy way St. Francis
whispered protection, the way I whisper trust.
My mouth fills with rain and I write you again.

My feet are twigs come to a mysterious end.
You will be denounced for not flinging her back
into woodland. None of us should be spared
winter. You pose her, a tattered queen among
sea grass and bluff clover. Written on the edge
of a cliff my story lies for all the world to read.

After My Grandmother's Love Letters

for Hart Crane

What cannot letters inspire? It is a dangerous
and contagious disease.
              —Heloise and Abelard

Poet, what made me do it on that April morning, leaning
across the railing of the ship, surrounded by souls,

my grandmother's love letters rising in a wisp of fog,
lanky suitors—one with a serious moustache, his eyes

absinthe green and pitying. One or more are frail,
pigeon-chested, no substance, not one capable

of taking liberties, I feel one stroke my wrist, he tries
to quiet my pulse. Poet, I should be afraid; they ask

me to leave this place, to join them. Theirs is a second
chance, a salty womb, bright trumpets and angels.

Unadorned tendrils of Sargassum become our dreams,
how freeing to rest here. If letters are souls,

we have much to answer for. Poet, make an epistle
of yourself. Be adrift in your own music.

April in Moscow

after Billy Collins

A letter never sent is a kind of purgatory.
      —Chekhov

After Helsinki, the colors of Moscow entranced me, all those
shades of blood, so I spent morning after morning walking
or taking the metro, popping out of the ground, like a Warhol

Locust. Turning my face to the sun, I'd breathe in Red Square,
while I worked myself up to a steaming bowl of borscht.
I wished I had been a healthy beet instead of a caramelized

onion, clearly different than my bustling camerados.
I walked along whistling "America" or chanting a song of myself;
everyone smoked here, even five year old boys. I'd pass

waitresses flexing their tired calves after a shift, rings of smoke
rising off them like birthday candles. I'd pass bankers and
civil servants, uncomfortable in their ill-fitting suits. They

would have left their cubbies in a hurry, beds messy, a fly swatter
at the ready in a burst of sudden self-loathing. Sometimes,
I would pass an unsent letter by Chekhov, awkward in his papery

skin, clearly aiming for a mail slot. Once, I saw a gaunt smoker,
unsure, perhaps shy: he disappeared down a side street where
I heard keening. Another joined him and they fought in the alley.

Whoever had done them wrong was still waiting for an answer.
Distraught and tortured, they would never satisfy with a reply.
In all my travels, in all my years of departures or arrivals,

sad faces at railroad stations, nothing had prepared me for this.
I had denied all my life what I secretly knew inside, somewhere
someone was waiting for one of these smoky eyed dreamers

to show up, to appear out of the blue swinging a picnic basket
of answers to thoughts reluctantly silenced. I sit with a bowl of
tasteless roots, a few bitter potatoes, before I make my way to a

yeasty café with strong coffee. And why, the postman through the
 window will see me as he knocks at the neighbor's door, pursing
beet-stained lips, murmuring gibberish to an empty envelope.

Conquest

for John Feeley

A peace is of the nature of a conquest; for then both parties nobly are subdued, and neither party loser.
                                        —William Shakespeare

We are props of a sort, let's not forget it. From her tarot,
she draws The Chariot which follows The Lovers, the impulse

that pulls her out of the garden. They are the heroes
of their own story. Afterwards, beneath snowy twigs,

the rabbit's steady breathing. Closer to fir tree than human,
closer to the wilderness, darkness than to Saints, starlight

thumb-tacked to snow, the chariot as swift as reindeer.
This garden has gone entirely to seed. Imagine the creatures,

who have clucked their waters for her. Beaver and duck
who have thrown down their bodies like gauntlets. Snow

blankets the land with Russian-winter ermine. Meanwhile,
beneath the snow, the rabbit's breath rises.

Lady Macbeth's Ambitions

Place a barren scepter in his hands, but know I knew
you and what you were capable of, my son, even

before the forest dissolved into flesh and faces
of those oak trees leaned over our birthing bed.

My sisters at the cauldron coveted your fingers, birth
strangled babe—I made sure there were ten before

I gave you away. I, your fine Lady-mother knew
the danger of you, before you were born, even

in my suck-tempest—I knew. With you at my breast
I could smell blood in the darkness. Each ghost-child

who wandered through the halls wanted to play
with you, wanted indeed to be you. You were my own

Love's undoing, with you at my breast I was no longer
unsexed. I see a future, lands filled with pheasants,

lakes that smell of turtles and not blood. There
is no risk nor lust for greatness with men who are satisfied.

With you at my breast, I can hear my sister's chanting.
I looked at the world and covered my mouth.

I covered yours next with a ribbon lace veil,
diamonds, tear shaped, knowing his ambitions are as dull

as his balls. Knowing I would have to set the world
spinning, set his mind to his future as the next King.

Jabberwock: The White Queen

I shall begin by talking about battles, because I was born during
a surrender, and it is my privilege to retell this dreary epiphany.

Captured on the white mount, so too the raven watches over
the souls who fall bloody, but it all began when he told me it
wasn't a one-winged dove that I heard, but a white one, like me.

I am spider-worn and used, but a trickster with no compass and no
theme to guide me out of this curse. I invent him out of nighttime,

the way a hound can lead a man from a bog, the forest with its
ragged trees, some bearded-old not wise, or soft and springy-birch
and pushing up for air, so the fated acorns gifted him to me.

Just lately, I have forgotten how to breathe. Sometimes I skip
the important parts in my own crooked life. Just this morning,

when I dressed, my breasts parted, thorns overcame my broken
columns, I was to be a tattered paper-white garden. Vagrant bees
seemed to overtake my limbs, buzzing angry, my marble-skin

loosened and fell away. Wild roses that climbed and clung, hurt
me with their chatter— they had imbedded deep and ingratiated

themselves with their sweet-mother's milk revenge. Finally
they dropped, dead-headed and sour from too much sun.
Their milky petals bled, orange and red rain ordained me human

no longer Queen. My under-skin pierced, the flutter of wings
and bees lifted me, uprooted out of this messy place, this unruly

nest of leaves, all those altercations with the red-rose flowers. I
was prodded out like a bad tooth. No matter what you have heard,
a virgin is the stained glass all ladies want to become. But what

hand would release me, summon me out of this mysterious walled
yard? Consider a girl who keeps slipping off, going back to sleep

in the briars. A cats-eye stone is hidden for good luck, swaddled
in a denim pocket, safe for borrowing, not really for keeping.

Oracle

When his spirit came to me from the North, spouting
nose-gays and jealousies, all those manly pursuits, I knew

I was in trouble. Consider the words he left "make a pledge, for
mischief is nigh." Then consider my dilemma. Mischief?

What bored Tower-Damsel wouldn't want that? To some, even
his words are illegitimate. I rave a little. It is his words, not vapors,

that intoxicate my senses. Heady I become from those old taunts:
long Vowels and short A's. *Tarantula, monsoon, antler:*

I can bear it, if you can. Even the goats are mesmerized.
Let this be a lesson to all women and men who adore mortals

who have a way with words. We shall grow our hair long to stuff
up our ears. Sing: *tra la, tra la.* Let their gutturals be captured

into a potion-bottle we clamp down with a cork.
Once upon a time, a lavender vowel escaped and I was left pining

in a turret. I was left with goats and chickens that cluck and bray.
Fancy me, and my fine fashion sense; I've adorned my hair

with plumes. A warning: you mustn't let some randy-hoofed
mischief-man talk you into letting your hair down

permanently. No free man or woman wants to lose his way,
fall off the tower, take her first tumble.

Jabberwock: The Red King

You could say I will go out "bang" like a candle,
the moment the Red King opens his eyes. The air

over our head will dissolve into rain, I might not breathe
if I only exist in his brain. But think of it this way,

if he did invent me, as all of those cards thought,
at least conjure me wearing silk, a peacock-paisley

pattern and then invent me with Rapunzel hair, more
than a handful, enough for a brick-tower, enough to lure

our next ex-King. His snore, the Brothers said, was more
than a growl; it awakened the planet. How do they see me,

homely or pretty, do I raise a fist or hurry fearfully away?
Do they want me to eat the cake and become the size

of a mouse or have them grasping my ankles while I loom
over their roofs? Are we real or just another

King's lightning-tempest? The Red King's snores expel
into the air, see the ghosts rise from his lips, spirits

scatter from his unreasonable demands. Me? I choose
to believe six impossible things before supper.

I hold each one of his ghost-walkers by the hand.
We skip merrily away, slip into the next dreamer's morning.

Forest, Baby Blue

for Jewel

Every sorceress is a pragmatist at heart.
—Louise Gluck

While I busied myself, sweeping
nettles on the forest floor, hanging
pinecones (gutted and lit with fireflies)
a nemesis turned you into a reindeer.

I could say, it doesn't matter.
I could urge you on, thigh muscles
still sore from the last time you exposed me
to your buckish nature. You could easily
carry my weight through a sentinel of trees.
My hair rolling silver down
my breast while we part rivers,
make our own waterfall.

Instead, you look at me with mournful
eyes, beg retribution. An army of deer
pauses for you to join them.

The forest floor moves, trips us
with its mossy carpeting. I wonder
should I continue? I need to string cranberries,
throw moths into the air like confetti.
I need to coax an egret
to give up its egg for our supper.

The forest waits, birds stop their evening-song
to listen. The pine forest is an ocean
to row against.

It's late, vagabonds will look for a place
to sleep below canopies of hemlocks.
I strike a match on one of your antlers,
start a fire for us to sit around and tell tales.
My lovers are ghosts who will not leave
nor follow. See how they watch us, silently
condemning us with dead eyes.

There is only one star out tonight
and we are falling.

Lazarus Receives a Visit from his Sister Mary

We put Mary to work in the garden,
had her bury her fingers in the black earth
of Cyprus. Often, we heard her weep.
The foolishness of loving a man,
promised to God.

Her tears baptized white and scarlet petals.
We sent her to the market to sell
vegetables we had grown. She carried
her wicker basket against her tiny frame.
She struggled under the bounty of peppers,
and figs.

When he asked her if she loved him,
they both knew what he meant. After
the murder that darkened the skies on the hill,
she threw herself at the cross like a mad thing.

She made me burn her hair. I used a straight
knife, sharpened against a rock and cut it
with care. Her head on a table, I worried
it was her throat she wanted me to slit.
Her eyes were fevered with a strange grief
that is not of spiritual passion. It was then,
I understood why she had broken
into her moneybox, squandered perfume
to wash his feet.

But her hair, her beauty gone. All traces
of the act that made her sweet to us, lying
on the floor ready to be swept away.

It was yellow like a field of sun orchids.
It was a gold coin, waiting to be spent.

Shipwrecked in a Reel of Stars

The lulling of the sirens was bliss. And then
the wrench of ship and sound. As you lay in the wreckage,

showing skin like the pale belly of a freckled
starfish, I remembered selkie men and imagined

that this must be a sin. Your mother left
an almanac of all your truths and lies

written in her even hand and tumbled
as smooth as sand in shells around your head.

A petticoat of foam was crushed
around your feet. There was no future

there among the glass.
I stole a line from you that day and sold it.

My tongue is a slippery piece of pink
silk. Jealous soul merchants want it, and me too.

You knew my small frame would dangle
without shame in the shiver of those biting stars.

Your eyes glowed red and I answered
you with my crooked little heart.

The Goose Girl

after The Brothers Grimm

1. Goose Princess

When I was a princess turned goose turned back
into a girl, I had a mind. Then all I had were feelings.

The sun on my back, feathers pointing in the right
direction. My horse knew me even when I was in the yard:
court yard, hen yard, an animal knows all your inclinations.

Lord, shine the sun so I can feel your Benevolence. Even if
I am only human. You never lost me, really. If my horse

has the wisdom to know me three ways, surely the stars
you scatter will lead us out of here. How we will shimmer
falling through the clouds, thundering hooves, feathers

and the dust you have formed to make us so. Maybe
next time, I will bow to the nectar Gods, skittering

in my neon green frock, pausing at each red poppy
that calls my name.

2. Falada

I hang in the doorway, no longer my equine self, only
a symbol of escape. I am gossiping pelt, ready to spirit

the right soul away. When I seek animals in the night,
with what ease they scamper and unravel black wool

with sharpened rice-teeth. I remind them that they
could be in my place, given the right circumstance.
See them set the night aflame with their "strike anywhere"
matches gripped and roaring like lightning through

this house? We'll soon be free. I suppose it's something
she and I will each embrace, a one-time sighting

of a feathered crown, a V formation, she at the helm,
when all magic returns and the universe preens and aligns

its feathers. The earth's judgments sadden me, but
just as I speak from my nail, the bent edge of a star,

Solomon should divide the two halves of our princess,
just to separate fowl from beast. I shall escape through

the window, she straddling my feathered saddle,
as we explore the farthest reaches of our kingdom

before returning to earth, to an unlikely prince.

3. The Rival

October has done its mischief here already. I own
her bloody handkerchief, stuffed deep in my pocket. I burnish
silver and gold threads to compete with the sun and moon.

Evil lasts forever, this is the month to prove my point.
I arrange the backyard in the pattern of feathers, not suitable

for a goose. Chickadees, sometimes finches—
I've shooed the hummingbirds back to Mexico to darn round
poppies of light. Here there is only room for dark flowers.

You already know how this will end. Pine needles blanket
dead mice. Skunks feed off the compost pile, I've forbidden

all animals with any grace. Paw prints show how the night
survives. With the right light and makeup, I have convinced
the fools that I am pure, that all princesses are created equal.

The Blind Fisherman of Gibeon

Before I had language, when the earth
held me in her clutches
I was a row of jonquils
entertaining bees.

All buzzing around my eyes,
their empty sockets, the roar of lightning,
when the hairs on my wrists rose.

It was easy to speak in visions.
The burst of little suns
in my final moments.
I became as dark as the soil
where I buried bulbs.

Now I am left with fingers to feel
for petals that echo of color.
My wife has a face made perfect
by fingertips and longing.

I live beneath the planks
where light filters through.
I hold my line slack,
not positive of life in brackish waters.

I throw out my hook
again and again,
wait for a tug, a battle—
A fish to reel in, to bloody.

Green Woman

Long after the fruit rotted I stood under
the tree waiting for the green woman to appear.

I suspect that in every sense made holy
by circumstance or memory, she had been

my invention as I had been hers. We hunger for
youth, channel our babies into moss-laden cribs.

Somehow, our mothers' bodies are cleansed into
the wild wood. Her benevolent expression

is so unlike my own crooked desires. She clutches
my hands as if to still them, I could have been

that way once but now there are things I have forgotten
to tell you about myself, things that would make you

want to fall in love. Instead, these half-truths
make the nights cold, curled leaves skitter around me.

The apples at my feet are wizened—made bold
by territorial worms. I would like to be generous

and say that both of us turned out all right, but
how important is it for you to be my emissary?

While I sleep in snow, busy yourselves replanting
my story in an orchard of your own frivolous history.

Comrade

in memory of Adrienne Rich

The tree I split open, rushed me, all limbs
and sap, sad seeds wayward and determined

to stray and take root. Next year in spring,
there will be a new row of them, poised to break

into battle, their blossoms will cover the earth
with pink spirals of hope. For now, it is winter.

The eldest stretches its old limbs toward the sky
scattered with dandelion stars. I stand in the dark

blowing questions to the moon's unblinking eye.
I mustn't forget the tree I split open could roar

with sweet syrup if I tap into it this March.
I mustn't forget the worst that can happen already

has. In times like these—when we were not
allowed to speak so urgently of trees.

The Peacock

He likes showing off to his looking glass
menagerie of animals, his ten acres and a manse,
his brood of drab hens and his golden ass.
You can keep your rolled-out green expanse
of suburban trim; it's not for him. He preens
or struts regally for the other creatures to adore,
imagines tigers and spider monkey queens
all gasp and gape over his latest paramour.
Handsome cock. The weeping trees it seems
are the eyes of his lover. Like the legendary sweet
boy becoming thinner and thinner, he dreams
he hears his name cheered down every street.

Where's the unicorn who'll make his pulse race,
and absolve the lake for wrinkling his face?

The Soothsayer of Arican

When the sick, the lame come
to me, seeking miracles—wooing
destiny with my cards, my third eye
I only have to utter one word *no*
to drive their hopes into caves,
to relieve them of the weight
they carry, such is futility.

You were my hardest hand to spread.
We laid each other like ghosts.
All that winter, bitter and snowy,
the weather buried us under—
lifted my nightie, unsure
of our intentions. An old woman
rapped on my wooden door. We thought
it the wind, who would come out?
The note she slid—*Desperate, please.*
She bargained for my hour, and you
barely through, semen drying
on my leg went to brew tea.

These are never the right answers,
The Fool, The Lover, The Magician
all point to an eventuality without
your heart's desire. I knew this before
I was fey, was born with this wisdom.
Her hair to her waist was as silver
as my rings. Still I took her money,
and told her anyway.

Afterwards, I took you like a host
into my mouth,

drank you like holy wine.
We made a pact.
I would only give you answers
on a day
when you were no longer my heart's
desire and none of this mattered.

I would send a message, speak
your name into the down of an owl.
Hesitate only if the word were one syllable—
if we discovered that this had been *yes*.

Silk Routes

In widely separated countries two lovers arrive
at the beach. Shells washed up by a green ocean are hieroglyphs

whispered by waves. A name is woven into Sargasso ribbons
by loitering gulls. At a market on wooden tables

a woman spoons out cinnamon and cardamom, precise
measurements for the wealthy to trade. The stories

of these seeds and nuts are swallowed deep inside wooden
ships, the silks the women fashion begin as worms that

murmur collars of poems into cloaks, flamboyant as parrots.
Wax lights a path where a man walks alone, fingers preoccupied

with the spiral of a curved letter masqueraded as a shell. Stars
that haven't dropped into the ocean shift their magic and slowly

sputter out. Scurrying crabs weave shadows into mossy dark.
The man will feed chopped heads of fish to the scavengers that

came before. He points his love home to her attic filled with boxes
buried in moths, exotic silks pressed into tissue paper soft as webs.

After supper each will serve their totem crusts from an oily plate.
They will share offerings from a past damaged by whatever storm

will answer its name. Under this woman's eaves a nest laced
with twigs and droppings from a bird who spared himself the cold

and flew to the Mediterranean. She plants her garden by starlight,
sows a lopsided pattern of shell hearts: purple, pink and white.

About the Author

Laurie Byro has been facilitating "Circle of Voices" poetry discussion in New Jersey libraries for over 16 years. She is published widely in University presses in the United States and is included in an anthology *St. Peter's B List* (Ave Maria Press, 2014). Laurie garnered more IBPC awards (InterBoard Poetry Community) than any other poet, stopping at 50. She had two books of poetry published in 2015: *Luna* (Aldrich Press) and *Gertrude Stein's Salon and Other Legends* (Blue Horse Press). A chapbook was published in 2016 *Wonder* (Little Lantern Press) out of Wales. She received a 2016 New Jersey Poet's Prize for the first poem in the *Stein* collection and a 2017 New Jersey Poet's Prize for a poem in the *Bloomsberries* collection. Laurie is currently Poet in Residence at the West Milford Township Library, where "Circle of Voices" continues to meet.

www.ingramcontent.com/pod-product-compliance
Lightning Source LLC
LaVergne TN
LVHW051607080426
835510LV00020B/3168